Wildlife garden

Ursula Kopp

Hubble & Hattie

Create a home for garden-friendly animals, insects, and birds

Hubble & Hattie

The Hubble & Hattie imprint was launched in 2009, and is named in memory of two very special Westie sisters owned by Veloce's proprietors. Since the first book, many more have been added to the list, all with the same underlying objective: to be of real benefit to the species they cover, at the same time promoting compassion, understanding and respect between all animals (including human ones!) Hubble & Hattie is the home of a range of books that cover all-things animal, produced to the same high quality of content and presentation as our motoring books, and offering the same great value for money.

www.hubbleandhattie.com

Photo credits: *Steinberger:* Front cover right hand side, rear cover top left & top right, pp 4, 6, 9, 10, 12/13 (top), 14-16, 18, 21 (all), 24-26, 29/30, 32, 34 (bottom L & R, top right), 35 top), 37 (both); *Strauß:* Rear book cover top middle, pp 28, 34 (top left), 35 (bottom), 36; *Wothe:* Front cover LH side 1, 5, rear cover bottom row, pp 11 (both), 13 (bottom), 39, 44, 46-56, 58-72, 76/77.

© 2019 Originally published in German by HEEL Verlag GmbH. Germany, under the title *Nütlinge im Garten: Anlocken, Ansiedeln, Einsetzen*, by Ursula Kopp. This edition published May 2020 by Veloce Publishing Ltd, Veloce House, Parkway Farm Business Park, Middle Farm Way, Poundbury, Dorchester DT1 3AR, England Fax 01305 250479/e-mail info@hubbleandhattie.com/web www.hubbleandhattie.com. © Veloce Publishing Ltd 2020 ISBN: 978-1-787116-00-9 UPC: 6-36847-01600-5

CONTENTS

Introduction

Today, the threat of global mass extinction of bees, and the alarming decline in many native bird species are key topics of discussion, including in our mainstream media. Intensive cultivation of mono-cultures and the wide-scale use of pesticides – which, in turn lead to destruction of traditional habitats and the various food sources they provide – are considered possible causes of this sorry state. We know that if just one species in a food chain is lost – and thus no longer able to perform its particular function – this will inevitably lead to the extinction of further species, and a reduction in the stability and productivity of the entire ecosystem.

The preservation of biological diversity is guaranteed only if pollinators are able to survive – and each of us can contribute to supporting and strengthening them. As an important first step, the use of pesticides should be avoided, and, in addition, local authorities and farmers should increasingly focus on planting green strips, wild meadows and flowers, and leaving flower strips to grow at field edges.

In city environments in particular, gardens now represent a refuge and substitute habitat for a diverse range of animal species: sometimes, they are the animals' last chance at a safe haven.

At the same time, many small and inconspicuous garden animals are only noticeable if they occur in large numbers, or become clearly visible due to feeding damage. Once this happens, garden owners are quick to talk of pest infestation, and turn to chemical remedies, ignoring the enormous damage this can cause to the garden's biological balance. With this in mind, anyone wishing to garden in a natural way should not only be aware of what lives in their garden, but also take this species diversity into account when planting and designing it.

This book is intended to help natural gardeners look out for common 'gardeners' friends,' and help them settle and thrive. The second part of the book contains detailed portraits of the most important and commonly-occurring garden helpers, with information on their way of life, nutrition and ecological requirements. In addition to providing practical advice, garden design ideas and instructions for building habitats and nesting aids, the book offers tips on how to attract and actively support as many of these useful species as possible. In doing so, gardeners can help ensure that the interaction of soil, plants and animal helpers produces an oasis for people and garden creatures alike.

An inviting environment for gardeners' friends

In order for gardeners' friends to feel at home, it's important that their living conditions are favourable. If your garden is dominated by lawns, with isolated plants scattered here and there, it won't be very effective at attracting garden helpers. If, on the other hand, your garden is alive with shrubs and flowering perennials, this greatly increases the number of available habitats and food sources.

Hedges provide space for birds, who readily feast on the various insects who live and feed there. Sticks and piles of leaves help hedgehogs to hibernate safely, while a dry wall with cavities provides an ideal home for lizards. Flowering plants attract not only honey bees and bumblebees, but butterflies and other helpful types of creature. Maintaining a natural garden is vital for attracting and retaining as many garden helpers as possible.

CREATING A NATURAL GARDEN

The spirit and magic of a natural garden stems from the fact that it is not created by human hands, at least not in the usual sense, with a great deal of effort and expenditure. A natural garden is about creating an ecologically balanced slice of nature; one that is not shaped by external forces, but that works with what is already there.

The first thing to consider is existing ground conditions: the soil should be of a type typically found in your region. Once you've determined the soil characteristics, you should select plants that will grow there readily and without much maintenance. In practice, you'll find that these are almost exclusively native species. Look at the surrounding landscape: what type of plants do you see? The key to being a natural gardener is to plant your garden in such a way that it blends in harmoniously with the indigenous flora.

Once you've let nature guide your selection, the only thing that remains is to group and introduce the plants in a harmonious way – there's really not much more to it. To enable your natural garden to really take root, however, here are a few key rules to remember:

- A natural gardener should work in a manner that is mindful of nature and the environment, and should learn from observing processes in the garden

- A natural gardener should be patient, open to experimentation and willing to seek advice

- The key is to garden with nature, not against it. As such, a natural gardener should dispense with the use of mineral fertilisers and pesticides, and care for the garden in a gentle way, tweaking it where necessary, and supplementing only when this is beneficial

Mixed hedge with grasses, shrubs and perennials

A functioning garden contains countless components, each of which has an array of complex dependencies. As such, the central goal of designing a natural garden is to create as many interconnected living areas as possible.

If you want to attract butterflies, it's not enough to plant nectar-producing flowers: these winged creatures also need plants for oviposition (to deposit or lay eggs), as caterpillar food, and to provide safe havens for pupation and hibernation. In a similar vein, it's not enough to hang a nesting box for birds without providing safe hiding places, and access to water for the insects and soil organisms on which they feed.

A diverse natural garden offers food, shelter, living space and nursery space for a wide variety of animal species, from the earthworm to the hedgehog; the bumblebee to the great tit. The more interconnected the various garden elements, the greater the supply of potential habitats, and the more animal species will feel at home there. This, in turn, increases stability and biodiversity.

Wild hedgerows: colourful variety

Wild hedgerows are an ecologically valuable source of shelter and food for local wildlife. What's more, they stand out from ubiquitous evergreen single-variety hedges and are decorative all year round, delighting onlookers with colourful flowers in the spring, ripe, juicy fruits in the late summer and an adornment of bright foliage in the autumn. To top it off, they are undemanding and resistant to weather-related influences and pests.

The shrubs found in wild hedgerows are an important habitat, particularly for birds who feast most readily on hawthorn, blackthorn and wild rose. The fruits of the hawthorn provide sustenance for more than 30 bird species and 160 types of insect. During the summer, wild roses are an important feeding ground for bees, while in the autumn and winter, their rose hips provide sustenance for more than 25 birds, and almost 20 species of mammals. The undergrowth of wild hedgerows is home to many of the spiders and insects readily eaten by birds, while ground beetles, amphibians and hedgehogs seek shelter in the dense ground scrub.

A crucial element of a natural hedge – and one which has also become rare in nature – is the herbaceous fringe. Located under the bushes, this area provides the transition to an adjacent green area or flower beds, and is home to numerous insects and soil-livers. Fallen leaves should be left to compost where they land, and cutting scraps should be piled up under or next to the hedge. Soon, an impenetrable maze of branches, groundcover, grasses and wild perennials will form: an ideal place for hedgehogs and other small animals to flourish.

1 GUELDER ROSE

2 BLACKTHORN

3 HAWTHORN

Native wildflowers are a valuable source of food for wild bees, butterflies, and other insects

The natural beauty of a wildflower meadow

In a wildflower meadow, there's always something going on. Signs of life are everywhere: honey bees humming, bumblebees buzzing, and colourful butterflies fluttering elegantly from blossom to blossom. But it's not only a place of colourful activity and a feast for the eyes: in the long run, it also requires much less effort than a conventional lawn.

A vital element for a flower meadow to prosper is the nutrient content of the soil. While most wildflowers and herbs flourish in poor soil, garden soil tends to be rich in nutrients due to fertiliser and input of nutrients from the air. If the soil in your garden is too rich, remove the sward, loosen the soil, and work in some sand. The amount of seed you'll need depends on the size of the area. The type of seed you choose should be perfectly coordinated with your soil type and light/shade conditions, and purchased from a specialist retailer. Spring and autumn are the best times for sowing. The seed must be sprinkled lightly, rolled and kept moist for six weeks. Be aware that in order for a flower meadow to establish fully in all its colourful glory, it requires a certain amount of time to take root – and thus a good deal of patience from the gardener.

Allowing your garden to grow wild

A natural garden should always contain a few areas that are left to grow freely: a spot behind the compost heap that's left to its own devices; an area for depositing clippings and leaves; an undisturbed pile of stones in a sunny corner or a stack of deadwood in the shade. These wild corners are enormously important for the garden's ecological equilibrium. They're a space where nettles (an indispensable food source for many butterflies) can grow unhindered, and spiders, toads and ground beetles can hide in order to hunt snails and insects at night.

For many species, a stack of dead wood provides an ideal place to shelter

A dry stone wall not only brings structure to a garden, it also offers a diverse habitat for many species of animal

The dry stone wall: a place in the sun

Natural stone walls are very popular as a garden design feature. Often, however, the stones are grouted with cement – which makes them pleasant to look at, but rather impenetrable for plants and animals. Stone walls can only become an ecologically valuable habitat if the stones are stacked dry and loose, as this creates a variety of different-sized cavities that, in turn, provide shelter, nesting and breeding sites for a range of living creatures.

In addition to numerous insects, reptiles – including blindworms, sand lizards and wall lizards – use the cracks as hiding places. When they emerge, they can quickly increase body temperature by basking on the sunlit stones before going hunting. Suitable choices of plant for such a wall include stonecrop, houseleek, saxifrage, speedwell and thyme varieties.

Ideally, the wall should be oriented in an east-west direction.

A nature-inspired garden pond provides a welcome oasis for flora and fauna, and will captivate all with its individual character

The natural pond: elixir of life

Incorporating water in a garden doesn't only enrich it for human eyes; with a nature-friendly pond layout and design, numerous insects, birds and amphibians (including the frog) will be enticed into and around your body of water.

The minimum size for a stable pond community is 8-10 square meters, with a minimum depth of 50-60cm. Ponds are usually sealed with conventional pond liner.

On clear days, the pond should be lit by sunlight for at least 4-6 hours of the day. Direct proximity to deciduous trees is undesirable, since falling leaves introduce unwanted nutrients into the water, and promote algae growth.

The pond should ideally be dug with a curved outline, which helps it blend harmoniously with surrounding terrain. The edge of the pond (0-30cm deep) is home to a flattish marsh zone. The shallow water zone (30-50cm deep), the most ecologically interesting area, should be generously proportioned and, where possible, in the northern half of the pond to allow it to receive plenty of sunlight. The deep water zone (50-100cm deep) should lie roughly in the middle.

Since pond plants proliferate quickly, it's best to limit these to a few varieties. A sand-based substrate or a gravel-sand mixture should be used for planting. Avoid stocking the pond with fish.

With the help of their expandable vocal sacs, male frogs attract females with loud croaking during mating season

A natural garden is considered very easy to maintain, because much of the work is left to nature. Nevertheless, from time to time, some effort is necessary to keep it blooming and flourishing.

Since natural gardens tend mainly to feature native plants, they do not need to be irrigated regularly. The plants are adapted to the climatic conditions of the local area, and require additional water only in the event of prolonged drought; preferably rainwater from a water butt. Nutrients are provided solely in the form of natural fertilisers and compost. For newly-created gardens, some winter protection may be required.

Soil preparation

Soil consists of two parts: the subsoil, which goes right down to rock, and the usually darker surface soil (topsoil), which can vary in depth. A surface soil layer of 20-30cm is best for the growth of plants and soil life, since numerous micro-organisms are undergoing life-sustaining processes at this depth.

To get to know your garden properly, first determine soil type. A 'light soil' contains coarse-grained sand particles, is not mouldable, and runs easily through the fingers. It warms up quickly in spring and is easy to work with all year round, but does not retain water and nutrients as well as other types.

'Medium soils' are the type most commonly found in gardens, and usually referred to as loam. If this is your soil, you should be able to mould it into a ball. A medium or loam soil heats up more slowly than a sandy soil, but is better at retaining water and nutrients.

'Heavy soils' feel greasy or soapy to the touch, and can be moulded easily due to their relatively high clay content. Clay soils also store water and nutrients effectively. The disadvantage is that they are difficult to work with, and it takes a long time for the soil to dry out enough to be hoed, dug or levelled.

The type of soil will determine plant selection in a natural garden. Avoid making major changes to the soil and, instead, establish indigenous species typical to your region, which will give the plants a better chance of flourishing long-term. No one soil type is 'better' or 'worse' than any other; rather, the natural character of the soil simply needs to be observed when planting. That said, even in a natural garden, some varieties of wild herb are undesirable if planned species are to prevail. Read up on wild herbs to recognise the types that proliferate voraciously via underground sprouts.

If you throw leaves from the garden into your household rubbish, many nutrients will be lost from the natural cycle. Instead of gathering up the leaves and removing them, simply leave them alone (in many areas of the garden), or pile them around sensitive plants as winter protection

Caring for the soil

Falling leaves, withered flower heads and dead plant pieces can be left in the garden. Much like a mulch cover, they protect the ground from fluctuations in moisture and temperature, while also providing it with nutrients. Plants can be strengthened and supplied with additional nutrients via natural fertilisers such as compost, horn shavings and dung. In addition, barren soils can be improved with 'green manure' crops such as lupine, vetch or clover, the planting of which helps to loosen the soil and enrich it with humus. Some plants can even help deter pests, or provide the soil with nitrogen or nitrate.

Cutting

Most of the time, shrubs and hedges in a natural garden can be left to grow freely; they only need to be thinned occasionally, so that they do not over-age. The best time to cut wild shrubs and bushes is during the 'growing break' from October to March. Small shrubs, such as sage and lavender, can also be cut after they flower.

Once the flowering period is over, many gardeners cut back perennials to just above the ground. For wild perennials, this cutting back only becomes necessary once spring (and thus the budding process) has kicked in; when left over winter, the dead stems do not

cause a problem, can look beautiful, and, most importantly, provide insects with an ideal place to hibernate. For higher-growing stems, the flowering parts of the plants should be removed during the flowering period to promote a second bloom. The stems of some ground-covering perennials can be shortened by about a third after flowering to encourage the plants to become bushier.

Under the Wildlife & Countryside Act 1981 (as amended), it is an offence to:
• intentionally kill, injure or take any wild bird
• intentionally damage, destroy or take the nest of any wild bird while it is in use or being built (golden eagle, white-tailed eagle and osprey nests are protected all year round)
• intentionally destroy an egg of any wild bird
• intentionally or recklessly disturb certain wild birds or their dependent young while they are nesting (including disturbance of nesting young)

Although within the Wildlife Countryside Act no dates are legally stated between which hedges cannot be trimmed, cut, laid or coppiced, the main bird breeding season is recognised as being between 1 March and 31 July. Therefore, the risk of committing any of the above offences is increased between these dates

A natural garden is a place of change. Plants that dominate one year may disappear the following. Others flourish loyally and reliably ... but never in the same place twice. This constant change is part of their attraction, however, and natural gardeners often find themselves spending increasing amounts of time simply observing life in the wildflower meadow, the wild perennial bed, or the edge of a woody thicket.

There's nothing wrong with giving nature a helping hand by buying wildflower seeds or young plants. As you make your selection, however, be guided not primarily by personal preference but conditions where you live, otherwise, many species will disappear and the joy will be short-lived.

Perennials and summer flowers are beautiful to look at, bring life to the garden with their vibrant colours, and provide an opulent feast for insects. Robust, easy-care plants cultivated in cottage gardens over centuries, that have adapted to climactic and geographical conditions, often prove a sensible choice.

When thinking about suitable plants for a natural garden, herbs are worthy of special mention. Mostly originating from the Mediterranean region, these aromatic kitchen staples are characterised not only by their culinary properties, but also rich blooms favoured by a number of insects. Due to their origin, herbs prefer sunny spots with permeable, lean soil.

Your plant planning should be based on the following criteria:

- Plants should preferably come from bio-conscious nurseries specialise in in wild shrubs and perennials. If you don't have such a nursery nearby, they can be ordered and delivered

- Care must be taken to ensure that the plants are able to cope with the conditions of their intended location (for example, sunny, shady, dry or damp ground)

- Wild perennials grow in nature and are not modified by breeders or gardeners. They are robust and therefore require little care; however, they do have the potential to spread and displace one another. In this case, they may require some gentle management

- The best month for planting long-living flowers and herbs is May. Perennials can also be planted in other seasons, as long as there is no frost on the ground

1 CHICORY
2 ANISE HYSSOP
3 DOG ROSE
4 LAVENDER
5 FIRETHORN
6 BLACK ELDER
7 CORNFLOWER
8 YARROW

Whether or not bees can derive benefit from a plant depends, among other things, on the shape of its flower. In contrast to their wild relatives, many cultivated plants have socalled 'double flowers' that deny bees access to their food source. Be careful to use only single-flowered forms

BUSHES AND SHRUBS

English name	Botanical name	Blossom/fruit	Location
Bilberry	*Vaccinium myrtillus*	Green-white, May/June; blue-black, from July	Semi-shade; humus-containing, sandy soil
Black elder	*Sambucus nigra*	Creamy white, May-Oct; black-red from Aug	Sunny to semi-shade; nutrient-rich soil
Blackberry	*Rubus fruticosus*	White, May-Aug; blue-black, Aug/Sept	Full sun; humus-rich permeable soil
Blackcurrant	*Ribes nigrum*	Greenish-yellow, April/May; black from June	Sunny; humus-containing nutrient-rich soil
Blackthorn	*Prunus spinosa*	White, April/May; blue-black from October	Sunny; dry, chalky soil
Common barberry	*Berberis vulgaris*	Yellow, April-June; bright red from Sept	Sunny to semi-shade; slightly moist soil
Common juniper	*Juniperus communis*	Greenish, April/May; blue-black, Aug-Oct	Sunny to semi-shade; dry soil
Dog rose	*Rosa canina*	Pink, red, June/July; rose hips, from Aug;	Sunny to semi-shade humus-rich soil
Dogwood	*Cornus*	White, May/June; blue, from Sept	Sunny to semi-shade; humus-rich soil
Hawthorn	*Crataegus varieties*	White, May/June; red from Sept	Sunny to semi-shade; nutrient-rich soil
Rowan	*Sorbus aucuparia*	White, May/June; red, from Sept	Sunny to semi-shade; dry to fresh soil
Scarlet firethorn	*Pyracantha coccinea*	White, May/June; orange-red, Aug/Sept	Sunny to semi-shade; loamy soil
Sea buckthorn	*Hippophae rhamnoides*	Yellowish, April/May; orangey-red-yellow from Sept	Sunny; humus-rich, permeable soil
Wild privet	*Ligustrum vulgare*	Greenish, June/July; black, Aug-Oct	Sunny to semi-shade; nutrient-rich soil

PERENNIALS

English name	Botanical name	Blossom/fruit	Location
Anise hyssop	*Agastache foeniculum*	Light blue, Jul-Sept	Full sun; thrives in any soil
Bellflowers	*Campanula*	Bell-shaped, lilac-blue, white, June-Aug	Sunny to semi-shade; humus-cont fresh soil
Catnip	*Nepeta*	Mauve to lilac-blue, June-Sept	Full sun; loose, permeable soil
Common chicory	*Cichorium intybus*	Light blue, July/Aug	Sunny; dry, slight acidic soil
Common columbine	*Aquilegia vulgaris*	Purple, pink, white-blue, May/June	Semi-shade; chalky, humus-containing soil
Common dandelion	*Taraxacum officinale*	Disc-shaped, yellow, April-May	Sunny to semi-shade; nutrient-rich, humus-containing soil
Common sage	*Salvia officinalis*	Blue-purple, May-Aug	Sunny; permeable, chalky soil
Cornflower	*Centaurea cyanus*	Bright blue, June-Oct	Sunny to semi-shade; nutrient-rich, humus-containing soil
English lavender	*Lavandula angustifola*	Dark to purple-blue, June-Sept	Sunny; permeable, chalky soil
Foxglove	*Digitalis purpurea*	Pink to purple, June-Aug	Semi-shade; humus-rich soil
Garden cosmos	*Cosmos bipinnatus*	Ray florets, pink to purple, white, July-Oct	Sunny; permeable, not too nutrient-rich soil
Globe thistle	*Echinops*	Metallic blue or silver-white, June-Aug	Full sun; highly permeable soil
Orange coneflower	*Rudbeckia fulgida*	Golden yellow, July-Oct	Sunny; nutrient-rich soil
Oxeye daisy	*Leucanthemum vulgare*	Ray florets, white, May-Oct	Sunny; thrives in any soil
Yarrow	*Achillea millefolium*	Ray florets, white, pink, red, June-Oct,	Sunny; nutrient-rich permeable soil

23

Within nature's grand design, each animal is content to play his or her role. Only humans seek to assign meaning and purpose to everything we see, hence our coining of the terms 'friend' and 'foe' to describe our animal counterparts.

However, this classification is not biologically meaningful. An ecologically-experienced gardener takes 'friend' to mean all of the creatures who are useful to him in tending a garden: ladybirds, earwigs, hornets, green lacewings, hoverflies and tachinid flies. As a rule, these are natural enemies of the pests who harm plants and other creatures.

Within this category, a further distinction is made between 'predators' – who kill their prey – and 'parasites' who are dependent on a host organism and feed on them from within. The beetle is a typical example of the former; the ichneumon wasp a typical example of the latter

A smaller sub-set of insects and invertebrates – such as woodlice and wasps – do not pose any actual danger to plants and other creatures, but are disruptive merely by virtue of their presence. These are more of a nuisance than a threat to the garden's survival.

The caterpillar of the cabbage butterfly infests all kinds of cabbage

The caterpillar of the small tortoiseshell butterfly feeds almost exclusively on nettles.

The term 'pest' is assigned collectively to all organisms who limit economic gains from agriculture and forestry (storage pests and wood pests). In domestic gardens, undesirable insects are far and away the main culprits, due to damage caused to crops and fruit plants when the feed, and their infestation of flowering plants. The most common garden pests include aphids, spider mites, and butterfly caterpillars.

Around half the species found in a species-diverse garden are classified as neither 'friend' nor 'pest,' but nevertheless play an important role in the ecological balance.

Examples include the great green bush cricket and other varieties of grasshopper. Many butterfly species also belong to this group, since they cause no damage in small numbers, and contribute to the pollination of flowering plants. Their caterpillars serve

Ants are typically viewed as unwelcome garden visitors, but are useful as a barometer of garden health, and rubbish collector. On the downside, ants protect aphids (a garden pest) from predators, as they lap up the aphids' sugary excrement, or 'honeydew.' On the upside, ants consume plant-eating insects such as leaf beetle larvae and caterpillars. Ants can be discouraged naturally using certain fragrances, such as lavender, tansy and wormwood

Stone bumblebee on fringed gentian

as a source of food for various species of bird when rearing their young.

Also classified as 'gardener's friends' are the large number of small creatures living in the soil, such as springtails. These feed mainly on dead plants or other organic material. As small humus-formers, they make a significant contribution to enrichment of the soil.

Insect hotels & living spaces for gardeners' friends

Extensive farming, planting flowering plants, and use of pesticides have all contributed to the gradual eradication of open spaces, and thus the destruction of important natural habitats.

For wild bees, in particular, it has become increasingly difficult to find a suitable place to nest and winter. Unfortunately, without the work of honey bees, bumblebees, butterflies, caterpillars and lacewings, it is not possible for flowers, fruit plants and vegetables to be pollinated, or for pest infestation to be regulated in a natural way.

Many species require tree hollows, burrows or boreholes in dead wood in order to build their nests. In nature, these boreholes are created by beetles. In human-maintained gardens, these natural nesting and hibernation spots can be difficult to find. This is where insect hotels and nesting aids come in – and why they are greatly appreciated by gardeners' friends and other mini garden residents.

WHAT IS AN INSECT HOTEL?

An insect hotel is an artificially-created nesting and wintering site for particular 'garden-helper' insects. Insect hotels can be big or small; free-standing or suspended from trees and walls.

The name derives from their multi-level design, which is sheltered from above by a projecting roof-like structure. Individual insects can move into the insect hotel and 'rent' a room the whole year round, during which time the eggs they deposit will develop into adults. As such, the purpose of the insect hotel is to offer native insect species – many of whose natural habitats have now been almost completely eradicated – a safe space for young-rearing and wintering.

At the same time, these lodgings contribute to the protection of flora and fauna, promote ecological balance, and provide interesting insights into the ways of life of different species. It's not only classic garden helpers like bumblebees, wild bees, ichneumon wasps, sphecoid wasps and braconid wasps that can be seen here; rather, lacewings, hoverflies, rove beetles, ladybirds, earwigs and butterflies will all readily accept an insect hotel as their home.

Ready-made insect hotels are widely available at specialist retailers, either to stand or hang in the garden. If you'd like to build your own insect hotel, you can obtain detailed instructions from various nature conservation associations. An example hotel is featured on pages 30 to 31 of this book.

Dividing up and filling the compartments requires a certain degree of creativity

If an insect hotel is to be a viable nesting place for garden insects, and not merely a decorative feature, there are a few things you'll need to consider in advance. The first is that an insect hotel will never flourish if the surrounding area consists exclusively of sterile green lawn, or is lacking in trees and shrubs. Only indigenous flowers, shrubs, trees, pines, wild herbs and flower meadows will provide sufficient food to keep your guests hanging around. For optimal results, you'll need a garden with a nature-friendly design throughout (see the chapter Creating a natural garden).

Since insects favour heat, the insect hotel should, as far as possible, be oriented in a south or southeast-facing direction. It should also be placed or hung somewhere sheltered from wind and rain: nothing is worse for insect larvae and eggs than moisture, because this brings the potential for mould. With this in mind, it is also important that the hotel is not on the ground (due to potential contact with ground wetness), but slightly raised above it.

It is likewise crucial that it does not wobble or sway. If you're mounting the hotel on a wooden wall, it will usually be possible to affix the back of the hotel directly to the wall with screws; if mounting on a stone wall or tree, you'll usually need to attach hooks first. Taut wire or pre-drilled holes on the back of the insect house can be used to suspend it from the hooks (of course, care must be taken to ensure that the intended nesting places are not restricted or damaged by any screws or hooks. Also worth bearing in mind is that insects will need a free way of entry, which means it's not a good idea to locate the hotel directly behind a tree or shrub.

When screwing the hotel directly to a wooden wall, take care not to damage the nest holes

Even though insect hotels and their various compartments are intended to accommodate a variety of insects, wild bees, in particular, seem to favour them as homes. This is why they are occasionally also referred to as 'bee hotels.'

If you're lacking in time or handicraft skills, you can buy ready-made insect hotels in various sizes and shapes from most garden retailers. However, hand-made versions are more individual, and usually more visually appealing.

Particularly where children are involved, building a hotel can be a memorable experience, and a fun way to introduce youngsters to the idea of nature conservation. In both cases, however, attention should be paid to the quality of workmanship and material selection.

Hollow bricks, pipes or flower pots can be used to sub-divide the individual layers and compartments. These sub-compartments can then be filled with reed stalks, hollow plant stems, tree slices and clay bricks (both, ideally, with holes), branches, twigs, stones and wood shavings. Your imagination is the only limit!

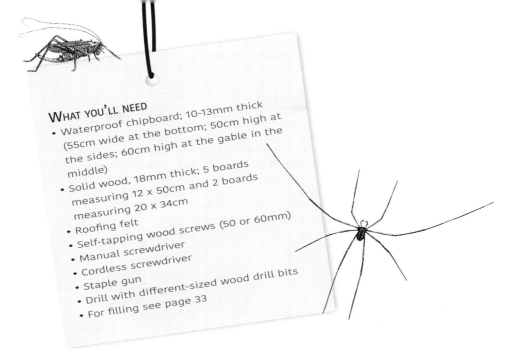

The instructions on this and the following pages will show you how to set up a five-star insect hotel with minimal effort: no specialist skills required!

The material for the insect hotel must be natural and free from pesticides, paint and solvents, and must not be pre-treated with wood preserver or hydrophobic coatings. The wooden parts can be obtained from any hardware store, where you can also have them cut to the desired dimensions.

- The long wooden boards serve as base plates, side panels, and shelves

- The two short wooden boards are used as roof tiles. The roofing felt can be cut to size and attached using staples or tacks

- The chipboard forms the back wall

WHAT TO DO
- First, assemble the base plate, side panels and dividing shelves using screws. The intervals between the dividing shelves will depend on what you plan to fill it with (bricks, tree slices, straw, etc)

- Then, screw the floor panel, side panels and dividing shelves to the rear wall. The roofing panels, which should be covered with roofing felt, can now also be fastened to the rear wall and the side panels

- The finished frame can now be secured to a wind- and weather-protected wooden wall, using two wood screws or screw hooks

THE FILLING

The bottom compartment of the model insect hotel on page 30 is filled with two perforated bricks.

The middle compartment contains three round slices of wood with holes (diameter 6-12mm, not quite bored through), with dry hay and straw nestled in-between.

The top compartment is filled with reed stalks and hollow plant stems, and its middle section is contained by a wooden board with boreholes (4-6mm). These holes provide an ideal place for wasps to build their nests.

To prevent birds pinching loose components/filling from the insect house, the entire front (apart from the bricks) of the hotel is covered with wide-mesh chicken wire.

Your insect hotel over the course of the year

March is the best time to install a hotel, since this is when the first guests tend to arrive Over the course of spring and summer, various species of wild bees will use the nesting tubes primarily to lay their eggs; however, they will also readily use them as shelter in bad weather, or as a place for hibernation.

Insect house with a filling of pine cones, drilled tree slices and bark pieces

In winter, the insect hotel should be left in its usual location, and must not be moved to a warm environment, since the insects and developing larvae hibernating there should only feel warmth (and thus be prompted to emerge from their hiding places) when spring arrives.

As a rule, the filling of your insect hotel never need be taken out and replaced completely. What matters is that it is wedged firmly in place, since every now and then, birds will make off with fir cones, pine cones, straw or reed stalks. Because of this, it's important to check regularly for gaps: the only way to prevent insect guests from rejecting your accommodation. Any obviously missing pieces can be replaced in the spring.

Spiders feed on insects, and, since they recognise the insect hotel as a rich potential source of food, orb-weaving spiders, in particular, will build their webs directly in the hotel's entry path. This means that freshly-hatched bees and wasps can become victims of a hungry spider on their very first flight. As such, the primary aim of keeping an insect hotel clean is to remove webs on a regular basis. Apart from this, very little maintenance is necessary. Damaged parts can be replaced in early spring, before the first tenants move in.

It's all about the furnishings!

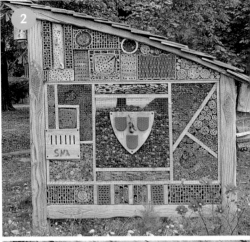

1 HOME-MADE INSECT HOTEL CRAFTED FROM WOODEN BOARDS, BRICKS, STRAW BUNDLES, RUBBLE AND NATURAL HEATHER MATTING

2 THIS LUXURY INSECT HOTEL, LOCATED IN A PARK, IS VISITED BY MANY DIFFERENT SPECIES

3 NESTING HOLES FOR WILD BEES DRILLED IN A PIECE OF BARK

4 TREE SLICES WITH A MIXTURE OF SEALED AND UNSEALED OVIPOSITORS (TUBES FOR EGG-LAYING)

5 THESE SPACIOUS LODGINGS CAN BE FILLED WITH BRICKS, STRAWS, PINE CONES AND KNOTS TO OFFER A COMFORTABLE HIDEAWAY FOR EVERY TYPE OF GUEST!

6 HOME-MADE INSECT HOUSE FILLED WITH PINE CONES, WOOD SHAVINGS AND MINI LOGS

7 COVERED WITH STONECROP AND SAXIFRAGE, A PILE OF STONES IN A SUNNY SPOT MAKES AN IDEAL RESTING PLACE FOR LIZARDS

A wire brush can be used to remove dirt, lichen and moss from natural wood collected from the forest

MAKING AN EARWIG POT

Earwigs devour aphids, spider mites and small caterpillars, which makes them a welcome addition to gardens.

A straw-filled pot provides these garden helpers with cosy sleeping quarters. The pots are populated from the beginning of May until late autumn. For best results, they should be hung in wind- and rain-protected areas of aphid-infested trees. If you want to locate the pot in a vegetable bed, place it over the top of a short pole.

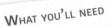

WHAT YOU'LL NEED

- Clay pot with hole
- Wood wool (alternatively, moss, straw or hay)
- 2 short sticks of wood
- String

WHAT TO DO

- Use the string to knot the sticks of wood together in the shape of a cross. Pass the other end of the string through the hole at the bottom of the pot

- Wedge the wooden cross inside the rim of the pot, to allow the pot to be suspended on the string

Earwigs like to be able to reach their shelter comfortably by foot, so they always need unhindered access. The pots must be suspended in such a way that they have direct contact with the trunk, branch or pole

- Now, add the filler material. The insects need space to move around, so avoid packing it too tightly. The wooden cross will stop the filling from falling out

- Securely suspend the pot from a branch

Hedgehogs begin a period of hibernation, approximately 4 months in length, from the end of October to mid-November. Because hibernation is determined by temperature and not season, a hedgehog may occasionally wake up during this period. When temperatures rise to between 12 and 6°C, the hedgehog enters a kind of 'half-sleep' – the phase in which the most energy is required. If the animal remains active while temperatures are consistently low, he will require extra help to get through the winter.

Building a hedgehog house

During winter, hedgehogs need a dry, safe place to shelter, and the most natural solution is to reserve a permanent space in a quiet, sheltered corner of the garden for a pile of leaves, a loose pile of wood, or a specially-prepared hedgehog house.

A hedgehog house looks a bit like an igloo, except that it's constructed from branches and foliage. It can be built relatively easily using materials readily available in the garden (cuttings, sticks, bark and stones), which should be arranged into a dome with a hollow middle and a clear, fortified access route. As a first step, the intended site of the house must be covered with sand or wooden boards and secured such that the cavity does not have direct contact with the ground, and is protected from ground moisture.

Small branches (60-70cm long) should be arranged around the ground covering, and the resulting interior space filled with leaves and straw. Finally, twigs can be laid as a roof and covered with a thick layer of leaves. Placing a small branch over the leaves will prevent them being carried away by the wind.

The hedgehog lodge should be about 80cm high, though interior diameter can vary depending on how the house is arranged. The entrance should be on the side facing away from the weather – to the south/east – and, if possible, be inaccessible to other animals.

From the outside, the shelter can be insulated with turf, brushwood or bark. Garden shops offer small pre-made 'igloos' that need simply be placed in a sheltered spot in the garden.

A garden that is nature-friendly and has good structural diversity has the best chances of recruiting many bird species as regular guests. Hedges, shrub patches and trees are especially inviting, but leafy climbing plants such as wild vine and ivy are also readily visited.

In a garden of this kind, birds can find enough food and shelter to build their nests and raise their young. Any lack of natural breeding spaces, especially for hole-nesting birds, can be alleviated by the provision of nesting boxes in the garden. Although these cannot completely replace natural hiding places such as woodpecker holes, aged knotholes or bark fissures, they are often the only way to entice birds into the garden to breed, and thus help them survive.

Blue tit with nesting material on a nesting box

Nesting boxes can be built from scratch using wood, or obtained from garden centres, etc. When setting up your nesting box, make sure it is inaccessible to cats. The entrance hole should be facing east, away from bad weather.

Opposite: A small, fortified entry point to a heap of leaves is enough to offer the hedgehog a secure place of retreat, and a winter home

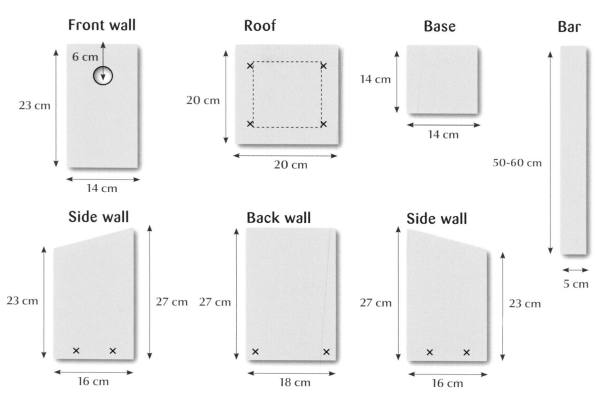

Front wall
6 cm
23 cm
14 cm

Roof
20 cm
20 cm

Base
14 cm
14 cm

Bar
50-60 cm
5 cm

Side wall
23 cm
27 cm
16 cm

Back wall
27 cm
27 cm
18 cm

Side wall
27 cm
23 cm
16 cm

Blueprint for a tit nesting box

WHAT YOU'LL NEED

- Spruce or fir wood boards from a hardware retailer; untreated, 2cm thick (for dimensions, see sketch)
- 25 nails (4–5cm)
- Hammer
- Wood drill
- Rasp
- Pencil
- Jigsaw

WHAT TO DO

- First, cut the boards to the dimensions indicated in the blueprint drawings. To do this, draw the outline with a pencil, then cut the wood using the jigsaw

- Next, roughen the outer and inner sides of the boards so that the young birds are better able to leave the nest. Before you begin hammering, it's a good idea to slot together all parts of the box without nails to ensure they fit

- Mark out an entrance hole of about 28mm diameter, and drill it into the front panel. The front panel should only be nailed to the side walls at the upper ends, to allow it to lift up when the box needs to be cleaned

- Now, nail the side walls to the back wall and base, and position the roof panel over the top. Check that the roof panel does not prevent the front panel from lifting before screwing it into place

- The bar for attaching the box should be placed in the middle of the back wall. The box should be hung 2-4m above the ground

- The box must be ready for occupancy by mid-March at the latest. It should be cleaned once a year (ideally September/October)

Nesting boxes for semi-hole nesters

While many species of bird nest primarily in closed nesting boxes, redstarts, black redstarts, robins, spotted flycatchers and blackbirds all prefer semi-open nest boxes. This is because they like to keep an eye on their environment when breeding and raising their young.

Nesting boxes for these semi-hole nesters should be hung in sheltered, quiet places, at a height of around 2-3m (no higher). The box should have a large, open entrance protected from the elements (rain and direct sunlight), and potential dangers (cats).

Semi-open nesting boxes can also be installed directly under the roof of a house in recesses, nooks and under protrusions. They should be cleaned more often than closed nesting boxes, since semi-hole nesters can breed several times a year.

Important gardeners' friends in portrait

The following chapter introduces the most important gardeners' friends: species that hobby gardeners may already recognise through frequent interactions, but which they might not realise are useful to the garden. The large number of species, in particular, shows how effective natural pest control can be.

The following portraits are intended to help gardeners identify these friends; make a realistic assessment of their importance to the garden; understand their habits and behaviour, and protect them and help them thrive.

Broad-bodied chaser *Libellula depressa*

Characteristics: The 4-5cm long abdomen is flattened, the male blue-grey with yellow spots on the sides; the female yellowish-brown. The four wings are longer than they are wide, and are spread to the sides at rest.

Habits and behaviour: Like their larvae, adult chasers feed on small insects; preferably mosquitoes and flies. After mating, the female casts the eggs onto the densely vegetated banks during flight. After about a month, the larvae hatch. Their period of maturity into adults, which takes two years, is spent entirely in the water.

Good to know: If a pond threatens to dry out, the larvae bury themselves in the mud, and can spend more than a month in a kind of 'dry sleep.'

Habitat and benefits

Broad-bodied chasers prefer clear ponds with few plants and a swampy substrate. if branches or stalks of plants protrude from the shore over the surface of the water, they often use these as 'hunting hides,' where they crouch in wait for nearby flying insects

Azure damselfly *Coenagrion puella*

Characteristics: Length of body 3.5cm; wingspan 4.5-5cm; males light blue, with a black, horseshoe-shaped marking on the second abdomen segment; females mostly greenish, with the upper side of the abdomen almost completely black.

Habits and behaviour: Mating and oviposition (egg-laying) take place on various water plants, when, you'll see many mating 'wheels' (see photo). Eggs develop within 2-5 weeks, and larvae overwinter in the water. Fully developed damselflies hatch from the beginning of May until end of August.

Good to know: During oviposition, the male anchors himself to the prothorax of the female, using an appendage on his abdomen, and stands stiff and upright, legs bent, over his partner, forming the signature 'wheel.'

Habitats and benefits

A calm, plant-rich pond is beneficial in persuading the azure damselfly to settle permanently in the garden. Pond plants should be varied, and should comprise some taller-growing species as 'hides' for hunting prey (mosquitoes and small insects)

Great green bush-cricket *Tettigonia viridissima*

Characteristics: 3-4cm long body is bright green, and often brown on the back; the wings, folded over the body at rest, protrude far beyond the abdomen, which ends – in the female – with a curved, sabre-like ovipositor (a tubular organ through which she deposits her eggs). Despite his long wings, the insect can fly only short distances of up to 100m.

Habits and behaviour: Active day and night, and at the end of the summer it's possible to hear him chirping from noon to midnight. After a fairly long mating period of up to 45 minutes, the female lays about 70-100 eggs into the soil.

Good to know: Sometimes, the insects climb into treetops and stay there longer than usual, chirping every evening in the same spot.

Habitats and benefits

The great green bush-cricket needs long grass, shrubs and trees as a hunting ground and refuge. He feeds on small insects, caterpillars and fly larvae. The young larvae like to eat aphids, which makes them very useful in the garden

European earwig *Forficula auricularia*

Characteristics: Body is about 2cm long, and red-brown in colour; wings are visibly stunted, and only partially suitable for flight. Inwardly bent pincers at the end of his abdomen are the earwig's trademark.

Habits and behaviour: The earwig is a nocturnal, photophobic (sensitive to light) insect. He feels at home in a damp, warm environment, and is often found under stones and planks, in wall cracks or piles of leaves. In autumn and winter, females lay their eggs in tree bark or burrows.

Good to know: The females run a tight ship when caring for their brood. After the eggs have been deposited, they are guarded by the females and defended against enemies. Regular turning and cleaning prevent dehydration, and protect from funghi.

Habitat and benefits

Earwigs will readily take shelter under large, flat stones or piles of deadwood. They are considered useful among gardeners because of their fondness for aphids and caterpillars

Seven-spot ladybird *Coccinella septempunctata*

Characteristics: The ladybird's 5-8mm long body is almost hemispherical. The head and chest are black with white spots; the hard, orange-to-bright-red wing cases (elytra) have 7 black dots.

Habits and behaviour: Larvae and ladybirds are found wherever their favourite food occurs – that is, aphids and scale insects. Adult ladybirds usually overwinter in groups under stones on the ground, in foliage or on plants at the edge of the garden. In spring and summer, they often travel from one location to the next in search of prey.

Good to know: In case of danger, ladybirds play dead: they allow themselves to fall and remain completely still.

Habitats and benefits

To keep ladybirds in a garden, leave one corner to grow wild (nettles are particularly welcome). Don't 'tidy up' areas under hedges too thoroughly in autumn. Ladybird larvae can eat up to 400 aphids a day during their development, while adult ladybirds can manage up to 200 per day

Golden ground beetle *Carabus auratus*

Characteristics: 2.5-3cm long, the head, pronotum (a prominent plate-like structure covering all or part of the thorax) and elytra are a shimmering, metallic green-gold; the edges of the elytra and pronotum are reddish-yellow. The legs are orange; the feelers (except for the first four reddish limb segments) are black. The elytra have 7 ribs.

Habits and behaviour: This predatory, daytime beetle is native to forests and meadows, but also occurs in gardens. During the day, he forages for prey on the ground. The black larvae, which appear at the end of winter, are also predatory, but are more active in the evening and at night.

Good to know: Once the beetle has seized his prey, he injects digestive juice, decomposing the creature's tissue, before killing it.

Habitat and benefits

Ground beetles hunt for grubs, caterpillars, slugs and snails, and kill more prey than they can eat. To tempt them into your garden, set up a protective refuge on the edge of a vegetable patch, with large flat stones, an old tree stump or pile of dead wood

Common red soldier beetle *Rhagonycha fulva*

Characteristics: This, the commonest species of beetle in central Europe, is 7-10mm long. The wings are soft and flexible; the head and breast reddish, with a black tip.

Habits and behaviour: In spring, the beetles appear in large number, and are eager flower visitors. They are often found on umbellifers, where they prey on other small insects and caterpillars; however, if necessary, they also eat leaves. The larvae are flat, brown or black-coloured, and spend the winter under stones or rotting plant material.

Good to know: The larvae remain active even at low temperatures, and will sometimes crawl across snow on warm winter days: thus, they are also known as 'snow worms.'

Habitat and benefits

These beetles love sunny areas and hedges: a flowering wild shrub hedge or a patch of tall grass will provide an ideal retreat. Sometimes they prefer to sit on leaves, where they feast on caterpillars

European rose chafer *Cetonia aurata*

Characteristics: A 1.5-2.5cm long, metallic, green-to-reddish beetle; two flat longitudinal ribs on the wings covers; white, narrow bands across the body in the rear third. On the upper side, the elytra are covered with longish, protruding hairs.

Habits and behaviour: From April to September these large beetles are often found in flowering shrubs and other flowering plants, primarily roses. The whitish larvae live in the soil, where they feed on leaves, rotting wood, and other organic matter.

Good to know: Rose chafers can rapidly take off for flight. They do not spread their elytra like other beetles, but keep them closed.

Habitat and benefits

A heap of leaves, preferably on a shady wall, is ideal for the beetle to lay her eggs. The hatched larvae produce high-quality compost soil, which can be used to enrich the soil of seedbeds

Wasp beetle *Clytus arietis*

Characteristics: The body is 7-15mm long; the black-and-yellow markings are reminiscent of wasps, and appear to give some protection to the beetle. The antennae become thicker and darker towards their end; the yellow line behind the shoulder is horizontal; the feelers and legs are red-yellow.

Habits and behaviour: These diurnal beetles can be found from May to June. They are very cautious: in case of danger, they will leave their living quarters immediately. Larval development lasts for two years, and takes place in dry branches of deciduous trees.

Good to know: If you catch a beetle in your hand, he will immediately try and scare his enemy – you – with loud chirping, produced by rubbing the front legs against the middle of the chest.

Habitat and benefits

Wasp beetles are wood recyclers, and will readily use a rotting tree trunk or stump as shelter. The larvae can also quickly decompose larger logs or stumps. The holes from which the adult beetles emerge are often used by solitary bees and wasps in which to build nests

Burying beetle *Nicrophorus vespillo*

Characteristics: 1.2-2.5cm long; the elytra have yellow and black bands; the three end segments of the antennae are yellow-red; rear legs are bent inward; the front part of the pronotum is covered with yellowish hair.

Habits and behaviour: Very sophisticated in caring for her brood, the beetle tracks carrion by smell, and uses digging and pressing motions to bury this in a tunnel leading diagonally underground. Oviposition occurs in a nearby tunnel, and she entices the young larvae to the carrion by chirping.

Good to know: Using organs located on the tips of their antennae, the beetles can smell dead carcasses from far away. Crawling beneath it, they dig the soil from underneath, causing it to sink into the ground; hence the name (they are also known as the undertakers of the animal world).

Habitat and benefits

Carcasses of birds or mice do not need to be thrown in the waste. Simply place them in a rear corner of the garden on a bed with loose soil, where, within a short time, they will be disposed of by carnivorous beetles

Common green lacewing *Chrysoperla carnea*

Characteristics: This delicate insect is 1-1.5cm long; the wings, which are translucent and intricately veined, have a span of up to 3.5cm; the compound eyes are golden, which is why the common green lacewing is also popularly known as a 'goldeneye.'

Habits and behaviour: These twilight and night-favouring insects sit hidden in foliage during the day. Oviposition takes place early in spring. The larvae are scarcely hatched before they begin to hunt for aphids.

Good to know: Some types of lacewing can communicate via ultrasound, which plays a role in their mating behaviour. The sounds are generated by twitching their hindquarters.

Habitat and benefits

Catnip is considered a good way to tempt lacewings into the garden, as they seem to be drawn to its fragrance. Wood shavings in a dry location are suitable as a wintering place. The larvae can eat up to 500 aphids during their three-week developmental phase

Peacock butterfly *Aglais io*

Characteristics: Peacocks have a rusty-red base colour, and wings with a span of 5.5-6cm. Their most distinctive features are the black, blue and yellow-coloured 'peacock' eyes on the tips of each front and rear wing, intended to scare off predators.

Habits and behaviour: After mating, females lay their eggs in batches of up to 500. After a week or two the caterpillars hatch and spin a communal web in which they live and feed on nettles. Before pupation, they disperse, looking for suitable locations.

Good to know: Adult Peacock butterflies drink nectar from flowers, and hibernate in tree cavities or sheds, which is why the peacock is always one of the first butterflies we see in the spring.

Habitat and benefits

In order to reproduce and develop, peacock butterflies need a nettle bush in a quiet corner of the garden. For butterflies who hatch in late summer, autumn blossoms (eg asters) should be planted as reserves for the winter

Buff-tailed bumblebee *Bombus terrestris*

Characteristics: The bumblebee's 1.4-2.3cm long, densely black-haired body has a yellow band on her breast and second abdominal segment; the final two abdominal segments are white.

Habits and behaviour: Buff-tailed bumblebees like open spaces, and frequently build their nest in abandoned mouse nests (*see also Habitat and benefits*). The queen excretes a substance that inhibits the development of fertile females and thus produces workers. If this substance is not released, the larval development takes longer and produces large queens.

Good to know: On certain flowers, the bumblebee beats her wings very fast, producing a buzzing sound whose vibrations release the flower's pollen.

Habitat and benefits

Buff-tailed bumblebees also build their nests in cavities in masonry and trees; where necessary, they will also use bird nesting boxes. Other options include a tall grass border, a pile of stones or a pile of wood in front of a hedge. The bees are particularly helpful in pollinating tomato plants, which would yield much less fruit otherwise

Garden bumblebee *Bombus hortorum*

Characteristics: The 1.8-2.5cm long body with elongated head is variably coloured, usually with three yellow rings on the chest and abdomen; the underside of the body is pale yellow; the abdomen is white.

Habits and behaviour: With their almost body-length proboscis, garden bumblebees can reach the lower-lying nectar in flowers. They prefer to build their nests under the surface of the earth, and pad them with moss. Once the winter is over, you can see the queens emerge very early in the spring.

Good to know: Only queens who hatch in the summer will overwinter after mating with a drone. Sadly, the rest of the bumblebee community perishes in the autumn.

Habitat and benefits

Bumblebees gather nectar and pollen from spring to autumn to raise their brood. Beds opulently-planted with sage, lavender and thyme are good at attracting bumblebees. Particularly effective is the early-flowering dandelion, which should always be left to flourish in the garden

European hornet *Vespra crabro*

Characteristics: With a length of 3-4cm, the hornet is the largest community-forming insect in our European animal world. He is black and yellow, with rust-red parts on the head, chest and legs.

Habits and behaviour: The hornet's preferred nesting places are dark locations such as hollow trees. The queen begins constructing cells in the spring as the basis for the first honeycomb. After 4-5 weeks, the first female workers hatch and build more of the honeycomb, plus a protective cover.

Good to know: Hornets are peace-loving, and seek primarily to preserve their own and protect the nest. A hornet's sting may be more painful than a bee or wasp sting, but is by no means more poisonous.

Habitat and benefits

As a sort of 'nature police' hornets play an important role in the ecosystem. A strong hornet will feed a pound in weight of mosquitoes, flies, aphids, moths, wasps and other insects to their brood every day. Their nests, built in hollow trees, on the ground or on buildings, must not be destroyed!

Grey-backed mining bee *Andrena vaga*

Characteristics: 1.3-1.5cm long; wild, black, hairy bee with a short proboscis; head and chest white-grey. At the base of the hind legs is an eye-catching bent tuft of hair.

Habits and behaviour: Like all wild bees, the grey-backed mining bee does not form a community. However, several females will socialise in a small area, sometimes with up to 50 nests per square meter. A nest consists of a 50cm-long main tunnel in the ground, with the brood cells located at the end. A distinctive heap of sand is piled up around the entrance.

Good to know: The male has no sting, and the sting of the female is so soft that it does not penetrate human skin.

Habitat and benefits

In order to determine where grey-backed mining bees settle in the garden, create a nesting area in a sheltered, warm spot where they will not be disturbed, and where visitors will not step foot too often. On average, the grey-backed mining bee pollinates twice as many flowers as the honeybee, and some types specialise in certain flowers

Hairy-footed flower bee *Anthophora plumipes*

Characteristics: With their 1.5cm long, compact and densely hairy bodies, hairy-footed flower bees are reminiscent of bumblebees, but can be easily distinguished by their much faster flight. The females are grey, brown or black-coloured; the males grey with a light head marking.

Habits and behaviour: Nesting is carried out preferentially in wall joints with clay and mortar. The over-wintering males hatch at the end of February, the females about three weeks later. The bee digs short nest tunnels. Each nest contains a number of brood cells, in each of which an egg is deposited.

Good to know: These bees have no need to defend a community, and behave peacefully accordingly. In contrast to other wild bees, they also have no appetite for sweet things.

Habitat and benefits

Spring-flowering plants and all kinds of fruit trees are popular food sources for bees who are already active. Due to their nesting habits, the bee also depends on artificial nesting options, such as dry walls with clay joints

Red-banded sand wasp *Ammophila sabulosa*

Characteristics: This slender, 1.5-1.9cm long, black digger wasp has a stalk-shaped abdomen that is thickened at the posterior; the end and basal segment are coloured red.

Habits and behaviour: Sand wasps are especially active during hot hours of the day, and hunt for caterpillars of butterflies and larvae of sawfly. The female digs through solid sandy ground by scratching with her forelegs, and creates a nest consisting of a 5-8cm long tunnel, ending in a horizontal larval chamber.

Good to know: The sand wasp drags her prey (eg a caterpillar) backwards into the tunnel, and lays her egg directly on the body. The larva hatches from the egg after a few days, and immediately begins to consume the caterpillar.

Habitat and benefits

The females suck nectar from flowers, and the males consume the honeydew of aphids. A bed of flowering plants is a welcome food source. A pile of sand in the corner of the garden or wood pieces with cavities work well as potential nesting sites

Marmalade hoverfly *Episyrphus balteatus*

Characteristics: The up to 1.2cm long, slender, dark green shiny body of the marmalade hoverfly bears black-and-yellow wasp-like bands. The typically fly-like head has distinctive big red eyes.

Habits and behaviour: The females lay their eggs directly on aphid colonies. The slippery whitish-translucent larvae hunt for aphids, which they pierce with their pointed heads and then suck.

Good to know: With its yellow-black colouring, the marmalade hoverfly imitates a wasp to protect against predators. However, the insect has no sting and is completely harmless.

Habitat and benefits

Adult animals suck nectar as an energy source and eat pollen for egg production, especially on umbellifer plants and plants of the daisy family. Adult hoverflies are keen flower visitors. They appear in large numbers with the first spring flowers, and can then be found on winter aconite cherry, coltsfoot, cornelian cherry, and willow catkin

Tachinid fly *Tachina fera*

Characteristics: A comparatively large fly (1-1.5cm) of typical orange colour; black bristles on the abdomen and black line down the middle, usually ending in a triangular point.

Habits and behaviour: The females lay their eggs in close proximity to caterpillars. The hatched larvae feed in a parasitic fashion, by drilling into the body of their host and eating him from the inside. The fully developed larvae pupate in the ground, and the following spring, the flies surface.

Good to know: Tachinid flies need sugar to fortify them, which is why they also drink the honeydew of aphids.

Habitat and benefits

The tachinid fly specialises in the caterpillars of owlet moths as prey, which are considered pests in a vegetable garden. Since this type of fly likes to visit flowers, you can tempt him into your garden by planting purple tansy and white mustard

Common earthworm *Lumbicus terrestris*

Characteristics: 12-30cm long and about 5mm around; the body has a red front half and pale rear half, and consists of up to 160 cylindrical segments, each with four pairs of short bristles.

Habits and behaviour: The nocturnal earthworm comes to the surface especially often in humid weather to collect seedlings, leaving them in tunnels underground, where they rot and later serve as food. After mating, the worm creates subterranean cocoons, where the young who hatch from the eggs develop. Earthworms consist of both male and female sexual organs, but cannot produce a whole new organism individually.

Good to know: Like a lizard, an earthworm can detach part of the rear body segment, leaving this for the predator as the worm makes off.

Habitat and benefits

To ensure that earthworms do not go hungry, leave fallen leaves in the garden, and place the compost heap directly on the ground. Earthworms make countless tunnels, which ensures good circulation and soil drainage

Brown centipede *Lithobius forficatus*

Characteristics: Length is 2-3cm; one pair of legs on each of the 15 segments. The first segment is merged with the head and, instead of a pair of legs, has a large pair of poisonous claws.

Habits and behaviour: These predatory nocturnal animals feed on aphids, spiders, the larvae of various insects and other arthropods. They find prey with their feelers, grip it and inject a fast-acting poison. The bite is also painful for humans.

Good to know: On their last two pairs of legs, brown centipedes carry a defensive gland with a sticky segment. In the event of threat, they can expel an offensive secretion from the gland, and may even be able to trap the attacker with the sticky segment.

Habitat and benefits

During the day, brown centipedes hide under stones, leaves, bark and stored wood. Since they are not fussy eaters, they devour almost everything that comes their way. This makes them valuable helpers with large-scale pest infestations

European garden spider *Araneus diadematus*

Characteristics: Like all arachnids, European garden spiders have a solid exogenous skeleton made of chitin. The body is 1cm long; the large abdomen is brown, marbled with a white, cross-shaped marking.

Habits and behaviour: When spiders grow, they have to shed their skin periodically. They immediately strip off the first layer after emerging from the egg, then shed several more times over the next few weeks. After the last shedding, they are sexually mature.

Good to know: The spider's big webs are little masterpieces of architecture. They require around an hour to weave an insect trap of 1m diameter. Only the spider knows which threads are sticky and which are not.

Habitat and benefits

Tall plant stems or low branches are necessary for web-building; climbing vegetables, shrubs in open areas or a tall grassy fringe can also be helpful. Since aphids, mites and other sucking insects account for up to 70% of their prey, garden spiders play an important role in the natural pest-baiting process

Common toad *Bufo bufo*

Characteristics: Up to 11cm tall, with a plump body, broad head and horizontal pupil and copper-coloured iris; colour usually brownish, grey or yellow; dry skin is covered with many large warts.

Habits and behaviour: Toads live in damp places and are active only in rain and at night. During the day, they rest under dead wood, leaves, stones or in self-dug holes in the ground. Every year, the females spawn 3000-6000 eggs in the same water; the young leave the water at the end of June.

Good to know: Once the toad has fixed his sights on suitable prey, his tongue darts out to capture the prey and transport this to his mouth in fractions of a second.

Habitat and benefits

If you want to attract common toads to your garden, offer them a natural garden pond with plant growth, and with stone or dead wood piles as shelter. Since these animals spawn vigorously, following generations are likely to return. The toad's favourite foods include slugs and potato beetle larvae

Common frog *Rana temporaria*

Characteristics: Body length is 9-11cm; top of the body colour is yellow/red to blackish-brown, often with largish spots; underside whitish-grey on the male and yellow-reddish marbled on the female. Hind legs have horizontal stripes.

Habits and behaviour: Common frogs are mostly nocturnal; for migration purposes as well as foraging for food. They typically deposit large collections of spawn in shallow water, often near the shore. Common frogs often overwinter in larger groups at the bottom of bodies of water.

Good to know: The frog's metabolic rate is kept to a minimum when overwintering; respiration takes place only via the skin. Cool water has a sufficiently high oxygen content to sustain the frogs during cold months.

Habitat and benefits

As with other types of frog, snails are top of the menu here, making the common frog a hard-working helper of natural gardeners. The frogs will feel at home in a rather less well-kept garden, with an uncut meadow, fallen leaves, rotting branches and stones. A pond in whose mud the frog can overwinter will also serve as a spawning site

Sand lizard *Lacerta agilis*

Characteristics: Up to 25cm long in total, the sand lizard's head and body combined are the same length as the tail; light brown base colour with variable pattern. The flanks mainly feature a dark band with light spots.

Habits and behaviour: The mating season begins at the end of April, and from mid-May to early August, the females lay up to 15 eggs in self-dug holes in sunny places. The young hatch from the end of July. Sand lizards hibernate in piles of stones from November to March.

Good to know: During the mating season, the males become a very bright green colour, particularly visible on the flanks and throat.

Habitat and benefits

The sand lizard readily consumes pests such as cabbage white butterflies and vegetable flies. In order to settle long-term, the diurnal sand lizard needs sufficient hiding places among heaps of brushwood, sand, wood, debris and shrubs. Sun-exposed, predator-sheltered places with high but sparse vegetation are essential in order to warm his body

Leopard slug *Limax maximus*

Characteristics: 10-20cm long, the leopard slug is brownish-grey with striking flecks and stripey markings (hence his name); thick feelers carry the eyes at the top, and are brightly coloured.

Habits and behaviour: Leopard slugs are hermaphrodites – that is, all individuals possess both male and female sexual organs. They are nocturnal, and only become active in wet weather, though you may also spot them on days that are overcast.

Good to know: Rarely seen, a gardener who does catch sight of a leopard slug will be cheered, because these effective snail hunters will even take on snails bigger than themselves.

Habitat and benefits

Ideal habitats are shady, moist spots under trees, with loosely piled hollow bricks and old wooden boards; these should be scattered with brushwood and rotting leaves. The animals move around in a 5–10 metre radius of their home. Because of this, it can be worthwhile placing their intended shelter centrally in the garden

Slow worm *Anguis fragilis*

Characteristics: Up to 50cm long, the head of this legless, slender lizard is barely distinguishable from the body and blunt tail; smooth, shiny scales; brownish or greyish on the upper side, underside yellowish on the male and grey to black on the female.

Habits and behaviour: Wintering in sheltered, frost-proof burrows, at the beginning of April, slow worms venture into the open. After mating, the female retains around 10 eggs in her body for 13-14 weeks, until they grow to around 10cm long; young hatch immediately after the eggs are laid.

Good to know: Like some of the other animals in this book, slow worms have predetermined breaking points along the body that allow the tail to be shed to aid escape in an attack.

Habitat and benefits

Since snails are at the top of their menu, slow worms are a firm fixture on the list of gardeners' friends. To persuade them to settle, a garden should not be too well-kept. They like to sunbathe on and shelter under stone slabs, and need access to a watering hole in summer

European hedgehog *Erinaceus europaeus*

Characteristics: At around 25cm in length, the hedgehog is a small to medium-sized mammal. Depending on body size, she carries up to 8000 brownish spines across her back and sides; short limbs; long, pointed, twitching muzzle.

Habits and behaviour: A solitary animal, active during night and twilight; climbs and digs well. During the day, the hedgehog hides away under piles of stone and brushwood, and maintains a nest well-padded with grass and foliage. Hibernation is from October/November to March/April.

Good to know: When in danger, the hedgehog rolls into a spiky ball to deter predators such as foxes, martens, cats or dogs. The tip of the snout pokes out of the ball to scent and determine whether the danger has passed.

Habitat and benefits

With a diet that includes slugs and snails, among other things, hedgehogs struggle in autumn and winter, especially the young who need to attain a certain weight to survive hibernation. Foliage piled in a well-protected place in the garden will provide shelter, or supply a self-built hedgehog house (page 38). Ensure hedgehogs have clear passage through your garden; they can roam up to 2km at night

Great tit *Parus major*

Characteristics: A migratory bird, the great tit is comparatively well-built at 12-14cm long. Head is black and white, underside yellow; male has a broad, black longitudinal band on chest and abdomen, which is narrower and paler in females.

Habits and behaviour: 1-3 broods (March-July); 6-12 white, red-brown speckled eggs are laid in tree cavities, nesting boxes, wall cavities and pipes, and take 8-12 days to hatch. Nests are made from moss, stalks, roots and wool; young emerge from the nest after 18-20 days.

How to spot this bird: Great tits are not shy, and are the most frequent dinner guests at winter feeding spots, from which they vigorously drive away other small birds.

Habitats and benefits

A valuable helper in pest control, Great tits are good at eradicating spiders, especially their larvae, and at distinguishing caterpillars from the bark of fruit trees. A breeding pair will hunt up to 8000 caterpillars for themselves and their offspring. However, while great tits might find enough food in the garden, sleeping and nesting sites are scarcer: hanging nesting boxes are usually warmly received

Great spotted woodpecker *Dendrocopos major*

Characteristics: A migratory bird, the woodpecker is some 23cm long; plumage is black, white and red, with striking white shoulder flecks and intense red tail; the male has a red head marking.

Habits and behaviour: A single brood (April-June); 5-7 white eggs are laid in tree cavities with a circular entrance, re-hollowed each year by both partners; incubation is 10–12 days. Young emerge after 21-23 days.

How to spot this bird: The bird ascends tree trunks in sudden movements, and uses his signature drumming sound to notify his territory. Fruit trapped in tree crevices are also an indication of his presence.

Habitat and benefits

In the summer, caterpillars, beetles and their larvae are the main food source, but aphids and ants, too; in orchards, this bird readily consumes the larvae of tortrix moths. She will only settle in the garden if she has trees for nesting – there or in the immediate vicinity. If a feeding station is placed near a fruit tree during the winter, this will likely bring the woodpecker back to the garden in the spring, since the larvae in the tree bark are a good source of food

European green woodpecker *Picus viridis*

Characteristics: Another migratory bird at around 35cm long; upper part and tail are green; crown is red, bright yellow rump; greenish-grey underside. The male has a red, black-edged beard strip; the female a black beard strip.

Habits and behaviour: A single brood (April-June), 5-7 white eggs are incubated for 14-16 days in self-built or adopted breeding holes in rotten trunks of deciduous trees; young emerge after 23-27 days, devouring countless numbers of ants before they leave the nest.

How to spot this bird: In winter, green woodpeckers dig their way through the snow cover in search of ants, creating distinctively-shaped holes.

Habitat and benefits

This bird hunts primarily on the ground, systematically scouring areas of grass. His favourite foods are ants and their larvae, and he also likes to plunder ant nests, which is why he visits open garden areas with short grass. To the delight of the gardener, the green woodpecker also retrieves codling moth caterpillars from beneath glue rings attached to the trunks of fruit trees to protect against pests

Eurasian wren *Troglodytes troglodytes*

Characteristics: One of the smallest birds in Europe (9.5cm), the wren has a spherical shape, and brown, slightly banded plumage with a light streak over the eye and a curved beak. Her short tail is usually acutely cocked.

Habits and behaviour: 2 broods (April-July), 5-7 whitish, delicately red-speckled eggs are incubated for 14-16 days in shrubs, spruce saplings, roots of fallen trees, tree cavities and wall cavities; the spherical nest is made of moss; the young emerge after 15-18 days.

How to spot this bird: The wren scurries silently like a mouse through the undergrowth. If foraging on the ground, this very lively little bird paces continuously back and forth.

Habitat and benefits

The wren's preferred nesting sites are old walls, ivy, dense shrub or thorny scrub. Occasionally, she will also accept semi-open nesting boxes. The wren is of great benefit to the gardener, because this skilful and vigorous feeder eats almost exclusively animal origin food: the larvae of cockchafers and leaf beetles and the caterpillars of undesirable insects, for example

Song thrush *Turdus philomelos*

Characteristics: A summer bird, the song thrush is 23cm long. The sexes are similar in appearance with warm brown upper parts, pale buff underparts with dark speckles (that look like arrows pointing towards the head and are often arranged in lines), and a tinge of golden brown on the breast

Habits and behaviour: Two broods (March-July), 4-6 light blue, black-dotted eggs eggs are incubated for 12-14 days in shrubs, trees or buildings; stable, cup-shaped nest made from moss and twigs, fortified with earth and mud; the young emerge after 14-16 days.

How to spot this bird: The song thrush shatters snail shells on a stone, tree stump or board in order to reach the soft body ('thrush's anvil'). He especially likes to sing in the morning and evening.

Habitat and benefits

The song thrush chooses dense, thorny shrubs for nest building. If shrubs bearing berries are present in a hedge, these will be a welcome additional source of nutrition – as will ivy berries that ripen in the spring. Above all, this garden helper has an appetite for caterpillars, mosquito larvae, slugs and snails

INDEX